POPE FRANCIS'
LITTLE BOOK OF
WISDOM

First published in 2015 by
Hampton Roads Publishing Company, Inc.
Charlottesville, VA 22906
Distributed by Red Wheel/Weiser, LLC
www.redwheelweiser.com

Published by arrangement with HarperCollins*Publishers* Ltd
Copyright © 2015 HarperCollins*Publishers*

Copyright © 2015 by Libreria Editrice Vaticana
Compiled by Andrea Kirk Assaf
Edited by Tony Assaf
Cover design by e-Digital Design
Cover photo credit: Pope Francis addresses the crowd on Easter Sunday, 2013 © Alamy.
Text design by e-Digital Design

ISBN: 978-1-57174-738-9
Library of Congress Cataloging-in-Publication Data
available upon request

Printed in the United Kingdom
10 9 8 7 6 5 4 3 2 1

MIX

Paper from responsible sources

FSC™ C007454

FSC™ is a non-profit international organisation established to promote the responsible
management of the world's forests. Products carrying the FSC label are independently certified
to assure consumers that they come from forests that are managed to meet the social, economic
and ecological needs of present and future generations, and other controlled sources.

Find out more about HarperCollins and the environment at **www.harpercollins.co.uk/green**

POPE FRANCIS'
LITTLE BOOK OF
WISDOM

The Essential Teachings

Compiled by Andrea Kirk Assaf

HAMPTON ROADS

Take this Gospel and carry it with you, to read it often, every day. Carry it in your purse, in your pocket, read from it often, a passage every day. The Word of God is a light for our path! It will do you well. Do it.

Pope Francis addressing the crowds after the Angelus prayer in St. Peter Square, March 22, 2015, after which homeless men and women distributed pocket-sized Gospels, a new Lenten tradition he began in 2014 to demonstrate that "the ones most in need are the ones who give us the Word of God."

Contents

A Note from the Editor

On Palm Sunday this year I happened to
mention to an Italian friend that I was compiling
quotes of Pope Francis for a small book.
Without missing a beat, he recited one of his
favorites to me, confiding that he often reads just
a sentence or two from one of the Holy Father's
writings or speeches so that he can reflect on
it for the rest of the day. He had been wishing
for a small volume of selected inspiring quotes
by Pope Francis that he could easily carry
along with him as he goes about his commute
and workday or during moments of leisure.

Sandro, this little book is for you, and for me, and for all who have found something beautiful, inspirational, and wise in the words of Pope Francis. May he continue to teach us and charm us with his surprises, wit, and wisdom for as long as the Lord chooses to bless us with his pontificate. May this little book allow Pope Francis to come along with us on our daily journeys as our confidant, fellow traveler, and guide.

Andrea Kirk Assaf
Easter Sunday 2015
Rome, Italy

PART ONE

Hope & Joy

Daily contemplation of the Gospel helps us to have true hope. Keeping our gaze fixed on Jesus is the core of hope.

To protect creation, to protect every man and every woman, to look upon them with tenderness and love, is to open up a horizon of hope; it is to let a shaft of light break through the heavy clouds; it is to bring the warmth of hope!

This is Christian hope: that the future is in God's hands.

[Y]ou have in your heart a promise of hope. You are bearers of hope. You, in fact, live in the present, but are looking at the future. You are the protagonists of the future, artisans of the future.

[F]reedom and hope go hand in hand ... wherever there is no hope, there can be no freedom.

Do not allow yourselves to be robbed of hope, and carry on! On the contrary, sow hope.

Christ is the one who renews every wonderful thing of creation; He's the reason of our hope. And this hope does not delude because He is faithful. He can't renounce Himself. This is the virtue of Hope.

Hope is the most humble of the three theological virtues, for it hides itself in this life.

It's best to not confuse optimism with hope. Optimism is a psychological attitude toward life. Hope goes further.

Hope is having our hearts anchored to our loved ones, our ancestors, to where the saints are, where Christ is, where God is.

[H]ope is not for one person alone,
hope is something we do together!
We must keep hope alive together, all of you,
and all of us, who are so far away.

There are difficult moments in life, but with hope the soul goes forward and looks ahead to what awaits us.

Anyone exercising a role of leadership—allow me to say, anyone whom life has anointed as a leader—needs to have practical goals and to seek specific means to attain them. At the same time, there is always the risk of disappointment, resentment, and indifference, if our plans and goals do not materialize. Here I would appeal to the dynamic of hope that

inspires us to keep pressing on, to employ all
our energies and abilities on behalf of those
for whom we work, accepting results, making
it possible to strike out on new paths, being
generous even without apparent results, yet
keeping hope alive, with the constancy and
courage that comes from accepting a vocation
as leader and guide.

We are all called to rekindle in our hearts an impulse of hope, that should result in concrete works of peace, reconciliation, and fraternity.

There is never a reason to lose hope. Jesus says: 'I am with you until the end of the world.'

Every period of history is marked by the presence of human weakness, self-absorption, complacency, and selfishness, to say nothing of the concupiscence which preys upon us all. These things are ever present under one guise or another; they are due to our human limits rather than particular situations. Let us not say, then, that things are harder today; they are simply different. But let us learn also from the saints who have gone before us, who confronted the difficulties of their own day. So I propose that we pause to rediscover some of the reasons which can help us to imitate them today.

For us Christians, wherever the Cross is, there is hope, always. If there is no hope, we are not Christian. That is why I like to say, do not allow yourselves to be robbed of hope. May we not be robbed of hope because this strength is a grace, a gift from God which carries us forward with our eyes fixed on Heaven.

Christian hope is not a ghost and it does not deceive. It is a theological virtue and therefore, ultimately, a gift from God that cannot be reduced to optimism, which is only human. God does not mislead hope; God cannot deny himself. God is all promise.

This is the joy which we experience daily, amid the little things of life, as a response to the loving invitation of God our Father: 'My child, treat yourself well, according to your means … Do not deprive yourself of the day's enjoyment' (Sir 14:11, 14). What tender paternal love echoes in these words!

The Gospel, radiant with the glory of Christ's cross, constantly invites us to rejoice ... Why should we not also enter into this great stream of joy?

No one can strip us of the dignity bestowed upon us by this boundless and unfailing love. With a tenderness which never disappoints, but is always capable of restoring our joy, He makes it possible for us to lift up our heads and to start anew.

Whenever our interior life becomes caught up in its own interests and concerns, there is no longer room for others, no place for the poor. God's voice is no longer heard, the quiet joy of his love is no longer felt, and the desire to do good fades. This is a very real danger for believers, too. Many fall prey to it, and end up resentful, angry, and listless. That is no way to live a dignified and fulfilled life; it is not God's will for us, nor is it the life in the Spirit which has its source in the heart of the risen Christ.

The joy of the Gospel fills the hearts and lives of all who encounter Jesus. Those who accept His offer of salvation are set free from sin, sorrow, inner emptiness, and loneliness. With Christ, joy is constantly born anew.

Joy is born from the gratuitousness of an encounter! It is hearing someone say, but not necessarily with words: 'You are important to me.' Saint Thomas said: '*Bonum est diffusivum sui*'—Good spreads. And joy also spreads. Do not be afraid to show the joy of having answered the Lord's call, of having responded to His choice of love and of bearing witness to His Gospel in service to the Church. And joy, true joy, is contagious; it is infectious … it impels one forward.

Technological society has succeeded in multiplying occasions of pleasure, yet has found it very difficult to engender joy.

We must restore hope to young people, help the old, be open to the future, spread love. Be poor among the poor. We need to include the excluded and preach peace.

The Gospel is the real antidote to spiritual destitution: wherever we go, we are called as Christians to proclaim the liberating news that forgiveness for sins committed is possible, that God is greater than our sinfulness, that He freely loves us at all times and that we were made for communion and eternal life. The Lord asks us to be joyous heralds of this

message of mercy and hope! It is thrilling
to experience the joy of spreading this good
news, sharing the treasure entrusted to us,
consoling broken hearts and offering hope to
our brothers and sisters experiencing darkness.
It means following and imitating Jesus, who
sought out the poor and sinners as a shepherd
lovingly seeks his lost sheep.

PART TWO

Faith & Prayer

Having faith does not mean having no difficulties, but having the strength to face them, knowing we are not alone.

The key that opens the door to faith is prayer. But it is one thing to pray, and another thing to say prayers.

One who believes may not be presumptuous;
on the contrary, truth leads to humility,
because believers know that, rather than
ourselves possessing truth, it is truth that
embraces and possesses us.

Faith is no refuge for the fainthearted, but something which enhances our lives. It makes us aware of a magnificent calling, the vocation of love. It assures us that this love is trustworthy and worth embracing, for it is based on God's faithfulness which is stronger than our every weakness.

Of course, we will never be able to make the Church's teachings easily understood or readily appreciated by everyone. Faith always remains something of a cross; it retains a certain obscurity which does not detract from the firmness of its assent. Some things are understood and appreciated only from the standpoint of this assent, which is a sister to love, beyond the range of clear reasons and arguments.

Faith is a path we walk with Jesus ... and it is a path that lasts all our lives. At the end the definitive encounter will take place. Certainly, in some moments along the path we will feel tired and confused. However, faith gives us the certainty of the constant presence of Jesus in all situations, even the most painful and difficult to understand.

Faith is not a light which scatters all our darkness, but a lamp which guides our steps in the night and suffices for the journey. To those who suffer, God does not provide arguments which explain everything; rather, His response is that of an accompanying presence, a history of goodness which touches every story of suffering and opens up a ray of light.

True faith in the incarnate Son of God is inseparable from self-giving, from membership in the community, from service, from reconciliation with others. The Son of God, by becoming flesh, summoned us to the revolution of tenderness.

With the eyes of faith, we can see the light which the Holy Spirit always radiates in the midst of darkness, never forgetting that 'where sin increased, grace has abounded all the more' (Rom 5:20). Our faith is challenged to discern how wine can come from water and how wheat can grow in the midst of weeds.

To live by faith means to put our lives in the hands of God, especially in our most difficult moments.

Crossing the threshold of faith means that we work out of a sense of dignity and see service as a vocation. It means we serve selflessly and are prepared to begin over time and time again without giving in to weariness—as if all that has been done so far were only a step on the journey towards the Kingdom, the fullness of life. It is the quiet time of waiting after the daily sowing and contemplation of the harvest that has been gathered. It is giving thanks to the Lord because He is good and asking Him not to forsake the work of His hands (Ps 138:8).

Crossing the threshold of faith means that we keep our eyes filled with wonder and do not let our hearts grow accustomed to laziness. It means that we are able to recognize that each time a woman gives birth to a child, it is yet another bet placed for life and for the future; that, when we show concern for the innocence of children, we guarantee the truth of tomorrow; and that, when we esteem an unselfish elderly person, we are performing an act of justice and embracing our own roots.

To have faith is to make space for God's love, to make space for His power ... for the power of the One who is in love with me, and who wants to rejoice with me. This is faith. This is believing: making space for the Lord so that He can come and change me.

Jesus is the Savior and we are saved by Him. This is the most important thing. And this is the strength of our faith.

Faith in Jesus Christ is not a joke; it is something very serious. It is a scandal that God came to be one of us. It is a scandal that He died on the cross. It is a scandal: the scandal of the cross. The Cross continues to provoke scandal. But it is the one sure path, the path of the Cross, the path of Jesus, the path of the Incarnation of Jesus. Please do not water down your faith in Jesus Christ. We dilute fruit drinks—orange, apple or banana juice—but please do not drink a diluted form of faith.

If we live the faith in our daily life, then our work too becomes a chance to spread the joy of being a Christian.

The Holy Spirit is the mover. This is why prayer is important. It is the soul of our commitment as men and women of communion, of unity. Pray to the Holy Spirit that He may come and create unity in the Church.

To be friends with God means to pray with simplicity, like children talking to their parents.

We all have our likes and dislikes, and perhaps at this very moment we are angry with someone. At least let us say to the Lord, 'Lord, I am angry with this person, with that person. I pray to you for him and for her.' To pray for a person with whom I am irritated is a beautiful step forward in love, and an act of evangelization.

I ask you all ... but reply in the silence of your heart, not aloud: Do I pray? Do I speak with Jesus, or am I frightened of silence? Do I allow the Holy Spirit to speak in my heart? Do I ask Jesus: 'What do you want me to do, what do you want from my life?' This is training. Ask Jesus, speak to Jesus, and if you make a mistake in your life, if you should fall, if you should do something wrong, don't be afraid. Jesus, look at what I have done, what must I now do? Speak continually with Jesus, in the good times and in the bad, when you do right and when you do wrong. Do not fear Him! This is prayer.

Miracles happen. But prayer is needed! Prayer that is courageous, struggling, and persevering, not prayer that is a mere formality.

To pray is to insist to the point of annoyance but also with an unshakeable certainty. Jesus feels our need when we pray and also feels that we are certain of His help.

Pray always, but not to convince the Lord by the strength of words! But as an expression of faith in a God who calls us to fight along with Him, every day, every moment, to overcome evil with good.

Do we truly pray? Without an abiding relationship with God, it is difficult to live an authentic and consistent Christian life.

Ask yourselves: 'How much space do I give to the Lord? Do I stop to talk with Him?' Ever since we were children, our parents have taught us to start and end the day with a prayer, to teach us to feel that the friendship and the love of God accompanies us. Let us remember the Lord more in our daily life!

In the face of so many wounds that hurt us and could lead to a hardness of heart, we are called to dive into the sea of prayer, which is the sea of the boundless love of God, in order to experience His tenderness.

PART THREE

The Church &
Evangelization

The Church is not a cultural organization but the family of Jesus.

May the Church be a place of God's mercy and hope, where all feel welcomed, loved, forgiven, and encouraged, the Church must be with doors wide open so that all may enter. And we must go out through these doors and proclaim the Gospel.

We need saints without cassocks, without veils—we need saints with jeans and tennis shoes. We need saints that go to the movies, that listen to music, that hang out with their friends (...) We need saints that drink Coca-Cola, that eat hot dogs, that surf the internet and that listen to their iPods. We need saints that love the Eucharist, that

are not afraid or embarrassed to eat a pizza or
drink a beer with their friends. We need saints
who love the movies, dance, sports, theater.
We need saints that are open, sociable, normal,
happy companions. We need saints who are
in this world and who know how to enjoy the
best in this world without being callous or
mundane. We need saints.

Our smallest gesture of love benefits everyone! Therefore, to live unity in the Church and the communion of charity means not to seek one's own interests but to share the suffering and the joy of one's brothers (1 Cor 12:26), ready to carry the weight of the poorest and the weakest. This fraternal solidarity is not a figure of speech, a saying, but an integral part of the communion among Christians.

We do not become Christians by ourselves. Faith is above all a gift from God which is given to us in and through the Church.

The Church must be a place of mercy freely given, where everyone can feel welcomed, loved, forgiven, and encouraged to live the good life of the Gospel.

The Church does not need apologists of its causes nor crusaders of its battles, but sowers humble and confident of the truth, who ... trust of its power.

You could say to me, 'But the Church is made up of sinners; we see them every day.' And this is true: we are a Church of sinners. And we sinners are called to let ourselves be transformed, renewed, sanctified by God.

The image of the church I like is that of the holy, faithful people of God … Belonging to a people has a strong theological value. In the history of salvation, God has saved a people. There is no full identity without belonging to a people. No one is saved alone, as an isolated individual, but God attracts us looking at the complex web of relationships that take place in the human community.

I prefer a Church which is bruised, hurting, and dirty because it has been out on the streets, rather than a Church which is unhealthy from being confined and from clinging to its own security. I do not want a Church concerned with being at the center and which then ends by being caught up in a web of obsessions and procedures.

Frequently, we act as arbiters of grace rather than its facilitators. But the Church is not a toll house; it is the house of the Father, where there is a place for everyone, with all their problems.

This church with which we should be
thinking is the home of all, not a small
chapel that can hold only a small group of
selected people. We must not reduce the bosom
of the universal church to a nest protecting
our mediocrity. And the church is Mother; the
church is fruitful. It must be. You see, when I
perceive negative behavior in ministers of the

church or in consecrated men or women, the first thing that comes to mind is: 'Here's an unfruitful bachelor' or 'Here's a spinster.' They are neither fathers nor mothers, in the sense that they have not been able to give spiritual life. Instead, for example, when I read the life of the Salesian missionaries who went to Patagonia, I read a story of the fullness of life, of fruitfulness.

The people itself constitutes a subject. And the church is the people of God on the journey through history, with joys and sorrows. Thinking with the church, therefore, is my way of being a part of this people. And all the faithful, considered as a whole, are infallible in matters of belief, and the people display this *infallibilitas in credendo*, this infallibility in believing, through a supernatural sense of the faith of all the people walking together.

The Church, which is holy, does not reject
sinners; she does not reject us all; she
does not reject us because she calls everyone,
welcomes them, is open even to those
furthest from her; she calls everyone to allow
themselves to be enfolded by the mercy, the
tenderness, and the forgiveness of the Father.

Spiritual worldliness leads some Christians to war with other Christians who stand in the way of their quest for power, prestige, pleasure, and economic security. Some are even no longer content to live as part of the greater Church community but stoke a spirit of exclusivity, creating an 'inner circle.' Instead of belonging to the whole Church in all its rich variety, they belong to this or that group which thinks itself different or special.

God save us from a worldly Church with superficial spiritual and pastoral trappings! This stifling worldliness can only be healed by breathing in the pure air of the Holy Spirit who frees us from self-centeredness cloaked in an outward religiosity bereft of God. Let us not allow ourselves to be robbed of the Gospel!

How often we dream up vast apostolic projects, meticulously planned, just like defeated generals! But this is to deny our history as a Church, which is glorious precisely because it is a history of sacrifice, of hopes and daily struggles, of lives spent in service and fidelity to work, tiring as it may be, for all work is 'the sweat of our brow.'

What does 'evangelize' mean? To give witness with joy and simplicity to what we are and what we believe in.

Practicing charity is the best way to evangelize.

If something should rightly disturb us and trouble our consciences, it is the fact that so many of our brothers and sisters are living without the strength, light, and consolation born of friendship with Jesus Christ, without a community of faith to support them, without meaning and a goal in life.

The joy of the Gospel is such that it cannot be taken away from us by anyone or anything (Jn 16:22). The evils of our world—and those of the Church—must not be excuses for diminishing our commitment and our fervor. Let us look upon them as challenges which can help us to grow.

What is called for is an evangelization capable of shedding light on these new ways of relating to God, to others and to the world around us, and inspiring essential values. It must reach the places where new narratives and paradigms are being formed, bringing the word of Jesus to the inmost soul of our cities.

The unified and complete sense of human life that the Gospel proposes is the best remedy for the ills of our cities, even though we have to realize that a uniform and rigid program of evangelization is not suited to this complex reality. But to live our human life to the fullest and to meet every challenge as a leaven of Gospel witness in every culture and in every city will make us better Christians and bear fruit in our cities.

Let us witness to the newness, hope, and joy that the Lord brings to life. Let us feel within us 'the delightful and comforting joy of evangelizing' (Paul VI, apostolic exhortation *Evangelii Nuntiandi,* n. 80). Because evangelizing, proclaiming Jesus, gives us joy. Instead, egoism makes us bitter, sad, and depresses us. Evangelizing uplifts us.

Listen well: 'Evangelization is done on one's knees'. Without a constant relationship with God, the mission becomes a job ... No. It is a not a job but rather something else. The risk of activism, of relying too much on structures, is an ever-present danger. If we look towards Jesus, we see that prior to any important decision or event He recollected himself in intense and prolonged prayer. Let us cultivate the contemplative dimension, even amid the whirlwind of more urgent and heavy duties. And the more the mission calls you to go out to the margins of existence, let your heart be the more closely united to Christ's heart, full of mercy and love. Herein lies the secret of pastoral fruitfulness, of the fruitfulness of a disciple of the Lord!

An evangelizer must never look like someone
who has just come back from a funeral.

When the Church loses ... apostolic courage, she becomes a lifeless church. Orderly, perhaps—nice, very nice—but barren, because she has lost the courage to go to the outskirts, where there are so many people who are victims of idolatry, worldliness, and weak thought ... Those who do not walk for fear of making a mistake make the most serious mistake.

A pastoral presence means walking with the People of God, walking in front of them, showing them the way, showing them the path; walking in their midst, to strengthen them in unity; walking behind them, to make sure no one gets left behind, but especially, never to lose the scent of the People of God in order to find new roads.

It is not creativity, however pastoral it may be, or meetings or planning that ensures our fruitfulness, even if these are greatly helpful. But what ensures our fruitfulness is our being faithful to Jesus, who says insistently: 'Abide in me and I in you' (Jn 15:4).

On the lips of the catechist the first proclamation must ring out over and over: 'Jesus Christ loves you; He gave his life to save you; and now He is living at your side every day to enlighten, strengthen, and free you.'

This is precisely the reason for the dissatisfaction of some, who end up sad—sad priests—in some sense becoming collectors of antiques or novelties, instead of being shepherds living with the 'odor of the sheep.' This I ask you: Be shepherds, with the 'odor of the sheep,' make it real, as shepherds among your flock, fishers of men.

Instead of imposing new obligations, (Christians) should appear as people who wish to share their joy, who point to a horizon of beauty and who invite others to a delicious banquet.

Before all else, the Gospel invites us to respond to the God of love who saves us, to see God in others and to go forth from ourselves to seek the good of others.

Nobody can go off to battle unless he is fully convinced of victory beforehand. If we start without confidence, we have already lost half the battle and we bury our talents. While painfully aware of our own frailties, we have to march on without giving in, keeping in mind what the Lord said to Saint Paul: 'My grace is sufficient for you, for my power

is made perfect in weakness' (2 Cor 12:9).
Christian triumph is always a cross, yet a cross
which is at the same time a victorious banner
borne with aggressive tenderness against the
assaults of evil. The evil spirit of defeatism is
brother to the temptation to separate, before its
time, the wheat from the weeds; it is the fruit
of an anxious and self-centered lack of trust.

The language of the Spirit, the language of the Gospel, is the language of communion that invites us to get the better of closedness and indifference, division and antagonism.

The Gospel tells us to correct others and to help them to grow on the basis of a recognition of the objective evil of their actions (Mt 18:15), but without making judgments about their responsibility and culpability (Mt 7:1; Lk 6:37).

But, careful! Jesus does not say, 'Go off and do things on your own.' No! That is not what he is saying. Jesus says, 'Go, for I am with you!' This is what is so beautiful for us; it is what guides us. If we go out to bring his Gospel with love, with a true apostolic spirit, with parrhesia, he walks with us, he goes ahead of us, and he gets there first. As we say in Spanish, *nos primerea*. By now you know what I mean by this. It is the same thing that the

Bible tells us. In the Bible, the Lord says: I am like the flower of the almond. Why? Because that is the first flower to blossom in the spring. He is always the first! This is fundamental for us: God is always ahead of us! When we think about going far away, to an extreme outskirt, we may be a bit afraid, but in fact God is already there. Jesus is waiting for us in the hearts of our brothers and sisters, in their wounded bodies, in their hardships, in their lack of faith.

It is urgently necessary to find new forms and new ways to ensure that God's grace may touch the heart of every man and of every woman and lead them to Him. We are all simple but important instruments of His; we have not received the gift of faith to keep it hidden, but, rather, to spread it so that it can illumine a great many of our brethren on their journey.

May the [Holy Spirit] give to all of us apostolic fervor; may He also give us the grace to feel uncomfortable about certain aspects of the Church which are too relaxed; the grace to go forward to the existential outskirts. The Church is in great need of this! Not only in faraway lands, in young churches, to peoples who do not yet know Jesus Christ. But here in the city, right in the city, we need Jesus Christ's message.

Every form of catechesis would do well to attend to the 'way of beauty' (*via pulchritudinis*). Proclaiming Christ means showing that to believe in and to follow Him is not only something right and true, but also something beautiful, capable of filling life with new splendor and profound joy, even in the midst of difficulties. Every expression of true beauty can

thus be acknowledged as a path leading to an
encounter with the Lord Jesus. This has nothing
to do with fostering an aesthetic relativism which
would downplay the inseparable bond between
truth, goodness, and beauty, but rather a renewed
esteem for beauty as a means of touching
the human heart and enabling the truth and
goodness of the Risen Christ to radiate within it.

Going out to others in order to reach the fringes of humanity does not mean rushing out aimlessly into the world. Often it is better simply to slow down, to put aside our eagerness in order to see and listen to others, to stop rushing from one thing to another and to remain with someone who has faltered along the way. At times we have to be like the father of the prodigal son, who always keeps his door open so that when the son returns, he can readily pass through it.

A missionary heart is aware of these limits and makes itself 'weak with the weak ... everything for everyone' (I Cor 9:22). It never closes itself off, never retreats into its own security, never opts for rigidity and defensiveness. It realizes that it has to grow in its own understanding of the Gospel and in discerning the paths of the Spirit, and so it always does what good it can, even if in the process, its shoes get soiled by the mud of the street.

The Christian ideal will always be a summons to overcome suspicion, habitual distrust, fear of losing our privacy, all the defensive attitudes which today's world imposes on us.

Holiness doesn't mean doing extraordinary things, but doing ordinary things with love and faith.

God calls you to make definitive choices,
and he has a plan for each of you: to
discover that plan and to respond to your
vocation is to move toward personal fulfilment.
God calls each of us to be holy, to live his life,
but He has a particular path for each one of us.

These are the two conditions in order to follow Jesus, hear the word of God and put it into practice. This is the Christian life, nothing more.

Therefore every vocation, even within the variety of paths, always requires an exodus from oneself in order to center one's life on Christ and on His Gospel. Both in married life and in the forms of religious consecration, as well as in priestly life, we must surmount the ways of thinking and acting that do not conform to the will of God. It is an exodus that leads us on a journey of adoration of the Lord and of service to him in our brothers and sisters. Therefore, we are all called to adore Christ in our hearts (1 Pet 3:15) in order to allow ourselves to be touched by the impulse of grace contained in the seed of the word, which must grow in us and be transformed into concrete service to our neighbor. We need not be afraid: God follows the work of His hands with passion and skill in every phase of life. He never abandons us! He has the fulfilment of His plan for us at heart, and yet He wishes to achieve it with our consent and cooperation.

The Christian is someone who can decrease so that the Lord may increase, in His heart and in the heart of others.

Let us protect Christ in our lives, so that we can protect others, so that we can protect creation!

Jesus does not force you to be a Christian. But if you say you are a Christian, you must believe that Jesus has all power—and is the only one who has all the power—to renew the world, to renew your life, to renew your family, to renew the community, to renew all things.

May we never get used to the poverty and decay around us. A Christian must act.

'When I want to do good, evil is close to me': this is the struggle of Christians.

If you grow accustomed to a life that is so-so, and you say: 'I believe in Jesus Christ, but I live as I want,' this does not sanctify you, it is not all right, it is absurd. [But] if you say 'yes, I am a sinner; I am weak' and you continually turn to the Lord and say to Him: 'Lord, you have the power, increase my faith; you can heal me,' then through the sacrament of reconciliation even our imperfections are taken up into this way of sanctification.

One important challenge is to show that the solution will never be found in fleeing from a personal and committed relationship with God which at the same time commits us to serving others. This happens frequently nowadays, as believers seek to hide or keep apart from others, or quietly flit from one place to another or from one task to another, without creating deep and stable bonds.

Genuine forms of popular religiosity are incarnate, since they are born of the incarnation of Christian faith in popular culture. For this reason they entail a personal relationship, not with vague spiritual energies or powers, but with God, with Christ, with Mary, with the saints. These devotions are fleshy, they have a face. They are capable of fostering relationships and not just enabling escapism.

I cannot imagine a Christian who does not know how to smile. May we joyfully witness to our faith.

Are we open to the Holy Spirit? Do we let ourselves be guided by him? Christians are 'spiritual.' This does not mean that we are people who live 'in the clouds,' far removed from real life, as if it were some kind of mirage. No! The Christian is someone who thinks and acts in everyday life according to God's will, someone who allows his or her life to be guided and nourished by the Holy Spirit, to be a full life, a life worthy of true sons and daughters.

And here the first word that I wish to say to you: joy! Do not be men and women of sadness: a Christian can never be sad! Never give way to discouragement! Ours is not a joy born of having many possessions, but of having encountered a Person: Jesus, in our midst.

The tasks of which Jesus speaks call for the ability to show compassion; our hearts are to be 'moved' and fully engaged in carrying them out. We are to rejoice with couples who marry; we are to laugh with the children brought to the baptismal font; we are to accompany young fiancés and families; we are to suffer with those who receive the anointing of the sick in their hospital beds; we are to mourn with those burying a loved one.

We are the friends of the Bridegroom: this is our joy. If Jesus is shepherding the flock in our midst, we cannot be shepherds who are glum, plaintive or, even worse, bored. The smell of the sheep and the smile of a father ... Weary, yes, but with the joy of those who hear the Lord saying: 'Come, O blessed of my Father' (Mt 25:34).

Jesus does not want us to follow a path of self-sufficiency. In order to be good Christians, we need to recognize that we are sinners. If we don't recognize that we're sinners, we're not good Christians. This is the first condition. But we must be specific: 'I am a sinner because of this, because of that ...' This is the first condition for following Jesus.

I never tire of repeating those words of Benedict XVI which take us to the very heart of the Gospel: 'Being a Christian is not the result of an ethical choice or a lofty idea, but the encounter with an event, a person, which gives life a new horizon and a decisive direction.'

When we say that a Christian is a spiritual being, we mean just this: The Christian is a person who lives and thinks in accordance with God, in accordance with the Holy Spirit. But I ask myself: And do we, do we think in accordance with God? Do we act in accordance with God? Or do we let ourselves be guided by the many other things that certainly do not come from God? Each one of us needs to respond to this in the depths of his or her own heart.

A final question: what can I, a weak fragile sinner, do? God says to you, Do not be afraid of holiness; do not be afraid to aim high, to let yourself be loved and purified by God; do not be afraid to let yourself be guided by the Holy Spirit. Let us be infected by the holiness of God. Every Christian is called to sanctity and sanctity does not consist especially in doing extraordinary things, but in allowing God to act.

There is a celebrated saying by the French writer Léon Bloy, who in the last moments of his life said, 'The only real sadness in life is not becoming a saint.' Let us not lose the hope of holiness; let us follow this path. Do we want to be saints? The Lord awaits us, with open arms; He waits to accompany us on the path to sanctity. Let us live in the joy of our faith, let us allow ourselves to be loved by the Lord … let us ask for this gift from God in prayer, for ourselves, and for others.

Sedentary Christians, lethargic Christians, will not know the face of God: They do not know Him. You need a certain restlessness to set out on this path, the same restlessness that God placed in each of our hearts and that brings us forward in search of Him.

A Christian life has to be defended and it requires both strength and courage. No spiritual life, no Christian life, is possible without resisting temptations, without putting on God's armor, which gives us strength and protects us.

The good shepherd, the good Christian, is outward bound, is always outward bound: he moves out of himself, he moves towards God in prayer, in worship; he moves out towards others to bring them the message of salvation.

Christians are men and women who bless. The Christian, through his life, should always bless, should bless God and others. We Christians are people who bless, who know how to bless. It is a beautiful vocation.

The 'yoke' of the Lord consists in taking
on the burden of the other upon oneself,
with brotherly love. Once you have received the
refreshment and comfort of Christ, we are called
in turn to become refreshment and comfort for
our brothers and sisters, with a meek and humble
attitude, in imitation of the Master.

We are not Christians 'part-time,' only at certain moments, in certain circumstances, in certain decisions; no one can be Christians in this way—we are Christians all the time! Totally!

The commandments are not a litany of prohibitions—you must not do this, you must not do that, you must not do the other; on the contrary, they are a great 'Yes!': a yes to God, to Love, to life.

Our life does not end before the stone of the sepulcher! It goes beyond with the hope of Christ who has risen! We are called as Christians to be watchmen of the morning, who are able to perceive the signs of the Risen One.

To be saints is not the privilege for the few, but a vocation for everyone!

Everyone is called, everyone is sent out ... The call of God can reach us on the assembly line and in the office, in the supermarket and in the stairwell, i.e., in the places of everyday life.

I urge you to serve Jesus crucified in every person who is marginalized, for whatever reason; to see the Lord in every excluded person who is hungry, thirsty, naked; to see the Lord present even in those who have lost their faith, or turned away from the practice of their faith, or say that they are atheists; to see the Lord who is imprisoned, sick, unemployed, persecuted; to see the Lord in

the leper—whether in body or soul—who
encounters discrimination! We will not
find the Lord unless we truly accept the
marginalized! May we always have before us
the image of St. Francis, who was unafraid to
embrace the leper and to accept every kind of
outcast. Truly, dear brothers, the Gospel of
the marginalized is where our credibility is at
stake, is discovered and is revealed!

PART FOUR

Love & Truth

Most people nowadays would not consider love as related in any way to truth. Love is seen as an experience associated with the world of fleeting emotions, no longer with truth. But is this an adequate description of love? Love cannot be reduced to an ephemeral emotion. True, it engages our affectivity, but in order to open it to the beloved and thus to blaze a trail leading away from self-centeredness and toward another person, in order to build a lasting relationship; love aims at union with the beloved. Here we begin to see how love requires truth. Only to the extent that love is grounded in truth can it endure over time, can it transcend the passing moment and be sufficiently solid to sustain a shared journey. If love is not tied to truth, it falls prey to fickle emotions and cannot stand the test of time. True love, on the other hand, unifies all the elements of our person and becomes a new light pointing the way to a great and fulfilled life. Without truth, love is incapable of establishing a firm bond; it cannot liberate our isolated ego or redeem it from the fleeting moment in order to create life and bear fruit.

The heart grows hard when it does not love. Lord, give us a heart that knows how to love.

Love shares everything it has and reveals itself in communication. There is no true faith that is not manifested in love. And love is not Christian love if it is not generous and concrete. A decidedly generous love is a sign of faith and an invitation to faith.

What is the law of the People of God?
It is the law of love, love for God
and love for neighbor according to the new
commandment that the Lord left to us (Jn 13:34).
It is a love, however, that is not sterile
sentimentality or something vague, but the
acknowledgment of God as the one Lord
of life and, at the same time, the acceptance
of the other as my true brother, overcoming
division, rivalry, misunderstanding, selfishness;
these two things go together. Oh how much
more of the journey do we have to make in
order to actually live the new law—the law

of the Holy Spirit who acts in us, the law of charity, of love! Looking in newspapers or on television we see so many wars between Christians: how does this happen? Within the People of God, there are so many wars! How many wars of envy, of jealousy, are waged in neighborhoods, in the workplace! Even within the family itself, there are so many internal wars! We must ask the Lord to make us correctly understand this law of love. How beautiful it is to love one another as true brothers and sisters. How beautiful! Let's do something today.

L ove is the measure of faith.

The secret of Christian living is love. Only love fills the empty spaces caused by evil.

Truth, according to the Christian faith,
is God's love for us in Jesus Christ.
Therefore, truth is a relationship.

True love does not pay attention to the evil it suffers. It rejoices in doing good.

The Apostle speaks of the love of God as the deepest, most invincible motive for our trust in Christian hope ... Even evil powers that are hostile to man are powerless in the face of the intimate union of love between Jesus and those who welcome Him with faith. This reality of faithful love that God has for each of us helps us to face our daily life, which is sometimes slow and tiring, with serenity and strength.

Everyone needs to be touched by the comfort and attraction of God's saving love, which is mysteriously at work in each person, above and beyond their faults and failings.

Saint Paul says that 'the love of Christ
compels us,' but this 'compels us' can also
be translated as 'possesses us.' And so it is: love
attracts us and sends us; it draws us in and
gives us to others.

Real power is love; love that empowers others, love that sparks initiatives, love that no chain can hold because this love is capable of loving even on the cross or on a deathbed. It has no need of youthful beauty, recognition or approval, money or prestige. It simply flows forth and is unstoppable. When slandered or defeated, it unquestionably acquires greater recognition.

We already know where the voracious greed for power, the imposition of one's ideas as absolute, and the rejection of those who think differently will take us: to a numbness of conscience and to abandonment. Only the commandment to love in all its simplicity—steady, humble, unassuming, but firm in conviction and in commitment to others—can save us.

The question of truth is really a question of memory, deep memory, for it deals with something prior to ourselves and can succeed in uniting us in a way that transcends our petty and limited individual consciousness. It is a question about the origin of all that is, in whose light we can glimpse the goal and thus the meaning of our common path.

PART FIVE

The Journey of Life

Life is a journey and when we stop moving, things don't go right.

The whole journey of life is a journey of preparation ... to see, to feel, to understand the beauty of what lies ahead, of that homeland toward which we walk.

Journeying is an art because if we're always in a hurry, we get tired and don't arrive at our journey's goal ... If we stop, we don't go forward and we also miss the goal. Journeying is precisely the art of looking toward the horizon, thinking where I want to go but also enduring the fatigue of the journey, which is sometimes difficult. (...) There are dark days, even days when we fail, even days when we fall ... but always think of this: Don't be afraid of failures. Don't be afraid of falling. What matters in the art of journeying isn't not falling but not staying down. Get up right away and continue going forward. This is what's beautiful: This is working every day, this is journeying as humans. But also, it's bad walking alone: it's bad and boring. Walking in community, with friends, with those who love us, that helps us. It helps us to arrive precisely at that goal, that 'there' where we're supposed to arrive.

I think this is truly the most wonderful experience we can have: to belong to a people walking, journeying through history together with our Lord, who walks among us! We are not alone; we do not walk alone. We are part of the one flock of Christ that walks together.

On the journey, which is often difficult, we are not alone, we are so many, we are one people, and the gaze of Our Lady helps us to look around us in a brotherly manner. Let's look at ourselves in a more fraternal way! Mary teaches us to have that look that seeks to welcome, to guide, to protect.

There is a deep and indissoluble bond between those who are still pilgrims in this world—us—and those who have crossed the threshold of death and entered eternity. All baptized persons here on Earth, the souls in purgatory and all the blessed who are already in paradise make one great family.

[T]here's also an ancient rule of the pilgrims, that Saint Ignatius includes, and that's why I know it! In one of his rules, he says that anyone accompanying a pilgrim must walk at the same pace as the pilgrim, not ahead and not lagging behind. And this is what I mean: a Church that accompanies the journey, that knows how to walk as people walk today. This rule of the pilgrim will help us to inspire things.

[Jesus] walks with the People of God, walks with the sinners; walks also with the arrogant.

B ut it is not enough to watch, it is necessary to follow! (...) Jesus did not come into the world to be seen ... it is a path and the purpose of a path is to be followed.

And now let us begin this journey, the Bishop and people, this journey of the Church of Rome, which presides in charity over all the Churches, a journey of brotherhood in love, of mutual trust. Let us always pray for one another. Let us pray for the whole world that there might be a great sense of brotherhood.

Those who believe, see; they see with a light that illumines their entire journey, for it comes from the risen Christ, the morning star which never sets ... Yet in the absence of light everything becomes confused; it is impossible to tell good from evil, or the road to our destination from other roads which take us in endless circles, going nowhere.

PART SIX

Family

The family is where we are formed as people. Every family is a brick in the building of society.

Like the Holy Family of Nazareth, every family is part of the history of a people; it cannot exist without the generations who have gone before it.

And I want to repeat these three words: please, thank you, sorry. Three essential words! We say please so as not to be forceful in family life: 'May I please do this?' 'Would you be happy if I did this?' We do this with a language that seeks agreement. We say thank you, thank you for love! But be honest with me: how many times do you say thank you to your wife, and to your husband? How many days go by without

uttering this word: thanks! And the last word:
sorry. We all make mistakes and on occasion
someone gets offended in the marriage, in
the family, and sometimes—I say—plates are
smashed, harsh words are spoken but please
listen to my advice: don't ever let the sun set
without reconciling. Peace is made each day in
the family: 'Please forgive me,' and then you start
over. Please, thank you, sorry!

Living together is an art. It's a patient art, it's a beautiful art, it's fascinating.

Holiness means giving ourselves in sacrifice every day. And so married life is a tremendous path to sanctity!

Some are called to holiness through family life in the sacrament of Marriage. Today, there are those who say that marriage is out of fashion. Is it out of fashion? In a culture of relativism and the ephemeral, many preach the importance of 'enjoying' the moment. They say that it is not worth making a life-long commitment, making a definitive decision, 'for ever,' because we do not know what tomorrow will bring. I ask you, instead, to be revolutionaries, I ask you to swim against the tide; yes, I am asking you to rebel against this culture that sees everything as temporary and that ultimately believes you are incapable of responsibility, that believes you are incapable of true love. I have confidence in you and I pray for you. Have the courage 'to swim against the tide.' And also have the courage to be happy.

Let us pray for peace, and let us bring it about, starting in our own homes!

In marriage, we give ourselves completely without calculation or reservation, sharing everything—gifts and sacrifices—trusting in God's Providence ... It is an experience of faith in God and mutual trust, of profound freedom, of holiness, because holiness presupposes giving of yourself with faithfulness and sacrifice every day of your life!

The three characteristics of Christ's love for His bride, the Church, are also at the heart of Christian marriage: faithfulness, perseverance, and fruitfulness. Christ himself is the model and measure of these 'three loves of Jesus': for the Father, for His Mother, and for the Church.

A family enlightened by the Gospel provides a school for Christian living! There one learns faithfulness, patience, and sacrifice.

The challenge for Christian spouses: remaining together, knowing how to love one another always, and doing so in a way that their love grows.

Mothers are witnesses of tenderness, dedication, and moral strength. Mothers are the ones who transmit the deep sense of the practice of religion, the first prayers, the first gestures of devotion.

Those who celebrate the sacrament say, 'I promise to be true to you, in joy and in sadness, in sickness and in health; I will love you and honor you all the days of my life.' At that moment, the couple does not know what will happen, nor what joys and pains await them. They are setting out, like Abraham, on a journey together. And that is what marriage is! Setting out and walking together, hand in hand, putting yourselves in the Lord's powerful hands. Hand in hand, always and for the rest of your lives. And do not pay attention to this makeshift culture, which can shatter our lives.

The life of a family is filled with beautiful moments: rest, meals together, walks in the park or the countryside, visits to grandparents or to a sick person . . . But if love is missing, joy is missing, nothing is fun. Jesus always gives us that love: He is its endless source. In the sacrament He gives us His word and He gives us the bread of life, so that our joy may be complete.

Sometimes it seems to me that, in our relationships with children and young people, we are like adults who abandon and disregard these little ones because they reveal our bitterness and our failure to accept old age. We abandon them to the vicissitudes of the street, with the attitude of 'every man for himself.' We abandon them to places of entertainment where they can amuse themselves. Or we abandon them to the cold and passive anonymity of modern technologies. We set aside our care for them, and we can imitate them because we do not want to accept our place as adults. We fail to understand that the commandment of love requires us to care, to set boundaries, to broaden horizons, and to give witness with our lives.

Life is often wearisome, and many times tragically so. We have heard this recently ... Work is tiring; looking for work is exhausting. And finding work today requires much effort. But what is most burdensome in life is not this: what weighs more than all of these things is a lack of love. It weighs upon us never to receive a smile, not to be welcomed. Certain silences are oppressive, even at times within families, between husbands and wives, between parents and children, among siblings. Without love, the burden becomes even heavier, intolerable. […] Jesus wants our joy to be complete! He said this to the apostles and today He says it to us. Here, then, is the first thing I would like to share with you this evening, and it is a saying of Jesus: Come to me, families from around the world—Jesus says—and I will give you rest, so that your joy may be complete. Take home this Word of Jesus, carry it in your hearts, share it with the family.

Family is the greatest treasure of any country. Let us all work to protect and strengthen this, the cornerstone of society.

Protect your families! Be living examples of love, forgiveness, and care. Be sanctuaries of respect for life, proclaiming the sacredness of every human life from conception to natural death.

Christians celebrate the sacrament of marriage because they know they need it! They need it to stay together and to carry out their mission as parents. 'In joy and in sadness, in sickness and in health.' This is what the spouses say to one another during the celebration of the sacrament and in their marriage they pray with one another and with the community. Why? Because it is helpful to do so? No! They do so because they need to, for the long journey they are making together: it is a long journey, not for a brief spell but for an entire life!

The perfect family doesn't exist, nor is there a perfect husband or a perfect wife, and let's not talk about the perfect mother-in-law! It's just us sinners …

[T]he 'home' represents the most precious human treasures, that of encounter, that of relations among people, different in age, culture, and history, but who live together and together help one another to grow. For this reason, the 'home' is a crucial place in life, where life grows and can be fulfilled, because it is a place in which every person learns to receive love and to give love.

The family which experiences the joy of faith communicates it naturally.

And they need Jesus' help to walk beside one another in trust, to accept one another each day, and daily to forgive one another. And this is important! To know how to forgive one another in families because we all make mistakes, all of us! Sometimes we do things which are not good and which harm others. It is important to have the courage to ask for forgiveness when we are at fault in the family.

Marriage now tends to be viewed as a form of mere emotional satisfaction that can be constructed in any way or modified at will. But the indispensable contribution of marriage to society transcends the feelings and momentary needs of the couple.

God's image is the married couple, a man and women, together. Not just the man. Not just the woman. No, both of them. That's God's image.

Christian spouses, celebrating the Sacrament of Marriage, make themselves open to honor the blessing of forming a community of life and love, entrusted with the mission to generate life, with the grace of Christ, for their whole lives.

Children are themselves a richness for humanity and for the Church, because they constantly recall the necessary conditions to enter the Kingdom of God: that of not considering ourselves self-sufficient, but in need of help, of love, of forgiveness.

The womb which hosts us is the first 'school' of communication, a place of listening and physical contact where we begin to familiarize ourselves with the outside world within a protected environment, with the reassuring sound of the mother's heartbeat.

May each family rediscover family prayer, which helps to bring about mutual understanding and forgiveness.

Children and the elderly are the two poles of life and also the most vulnerable, often the most forgotten. A society that abandons children and marginalizes the elderly severs its roots and obscures its future. Whenever a child is abandoned and an old person is marginalized, is not just an act of injustice, but it also demonstrates the failure of that society. Taking care of children and the elderly is the only choice of civilization.

Experience teaches us: in order to know oneself well and develop harmoniously, a human being needs the reciprocity of man and woman. When that is lacking, one can see the consequences. We are made to listen to one another and help one another. We can say that without the mutual enrichment of this relationship—in thought and in action, in affection and in work, as well as in faith—the two cannot even understand the depth of what it means to be man and woman.

In order to resolve the problems in their relationships, men and women need to speak to one another more, listen to each other more, get to know one another better, love one another more. They must treat each other with respect and cooperate in friendship. On this human basis, sustained by the grace of God, it is possible to plan a lifelong marital and familial union. The marital and familial bond is a serious matter, and it is so for everyone, not just for believers.

PART SEVEN

Building a Better World

All the wars, all the strife, all the unsolved problems over which we clash are due to the lack of dialogue.

It is my hope that interreligious and ecumenical cooperation will demonstrate that men and women do not have to forsake their identity, whether ethnic or religious, in order to live in harmony with their brothers and sisters. How many ways there are for the followers of the different religions to carry out this service! How many are the needs that must be tended to with the healing balm of fraternal solidarity!

God is peace: let us ask Him to help us to be peacemakers each day, in our life, in our families, in our cities and nations, in the whole world.

When leaders in various fields ask me for advice, my response is always the same: dialogue, dialogue, dialogue. The only way for individuals, families, and societies to grow, the only way for the life of peoples to progress, is via the culture of encounter, a culture in which all have something good to give and all can receive something good in return. Others always have something to give me, if we know how to approach them in a spirit of openness and without prejudice ... Today, either we take the risk of dialogue, we risk the culture of encounter, or we all fall; this is the path that will bear fruit.

It's important to not let too much time pass
after a storm, after a problem. It's important
to build dialogue as soon as possible, because
time allows the walls of resentment to grow
taller, just as the weeds grow taller and get
in the way of the corn—and when our walls
grow tall, reconciliation becomes so difficult!

If it is assumed that we all belong to human nature, prejudices and falsehoods can be overcome and an understanding of the other according to a new perspective can begin.

It is not possible to build bridges between people while forgetting God. But the converse is also true: it is not possible to establish true links with God, while ignoring other people. Hence it is important to intensify dialogue among the various religions, and I am thinking particularly of dialogue with Islam. At the Mass marking the beginning of my ministry, I greatly appreciated the presence of so many civil and religious leaders from the Islamic world. And it is also important to intensify outreach to non-believers, so that the differences which divide and hurt us may never prevail, but rather the desire to build true links of friendship between all peoples, despite their diversity.

The Catholic Church is aware of the importance of the promotion of friendship and respect between men and women of different religious traditions. I want to repeat this: *the promotion of friendship and respect between men and women of different religious traditions.* (...) [The Church] is also aware of the responsibility that we all bear to this our world, to all of creation, which we should love and protect. And we can do much for the good of the poorest, of the weak and suffering, to promote justice and reconciliation, to build peace.

A dialogue which seeks social peace and justice is in itself, beyond all merely practical considerations, an ethical commitment which brings about a new social situation.

Carrying on a dialogue means being convinced that others have something good to say, it means making room for their viewpoint, their opinion, their suggestions, without, obviously, slipping into relativism.

This is important: to get to know people, listen, expand the circle of ideas. The world is crisscrossed by roads that come closer together and move apart, but the important thing is that they lead toward the Good.

Each of us has a vision of good and of evil. We have to encourage people to move towards what they think is good ... Everyone has his own idea of good and evil and must choose to follow the good and fight evil as he conceives them. That would be enough to make the world a better place.

True openness involves remaining steadfast in one's deepest convictions, clear and joyful in one's own identity, while at the same time being 'open to understanding those of the other party' and 'knowing that dialogue can enrich each side.' What is not helpful is a diplomatic openness which says 'yes' to everything in order to avoid problems, for this would be a way of deceiving others and denying them the good which we have been given to share generously with others. Evangelization and interreligious dialogue, far from being opposed, mutually support and nourish one another.

Those wounded by historical divisions find it difficult to accept our invitation to forgiveness and reconciliation, since they think that we are ignoring their pain or are asking them to give up their memory and ideals. But if they see the witness of authentically fraternal and reconciled communities, they will find that witness luminous and attractive.

War is madness. Whereas God carries forward the work of creation, and we men and women are called to participate in His work, war destroys. It also ruins the most beautiful work of His hands: human beings. War ruins everything, even the bonds between brothers. War is irrational; its only plan is to bring destruction: it seeks to grow by destroying.

The time has come for religious leaders
to cooperate more effectively in the
work of healing wounds, resolving conflicts,
and pursuing peace. Peace is the sure sign
of a commitment to the cause of God.
Religious leaders are called to be men
and women of peace. They are capable of
fostering the culture of encounter and peace,

when other options fail or falter. We must be peacemakers, and our communities must be schools of respect and dialogue with those of other ethnic or religious groups, places where we learn to overcome tensions, foster just and peaceful relations between peoples and social groups, and build a better future for coming generations.

PART EIGHT

Listening to God

'God is love.' His is not a sentimental, emotional kind of love but the love of the Father who is the origin of all life, the love of the Son who dies on the Cross and is raised, the love of the Spirit who renews human beings and the world. Thinking that God is love does us so much good, because it teaches us to love, to give ourselves to others as Jesus gave himself to us and walks with us. Jesus walks beside us on the road through life.

This is to listen to the word of God, listen with your ears and hear with your heart.

What is the image we have of God?
Perhaps He appears to us as a
severe judge, as someone who curtails our
freedom and the way we live our lives. But
the Scriptures everywhere tell us that God is
the Living One, the one who bestows life and
points the way to fullness of life.

No one is more patient than God the Father; no one understands and knows how to wait as much as He does.

The Lord is very generous. The Lord opens all doors. The Lord also understands those who say to Him, 'No, Lord, I don't want to go to you.' He understands and is waiting for them, because He is merciful. But the Lord does not like those who say 'yes' and do the opposite; who pretend to thank Him for all the good things; who have good manners, but go their own way and do not follow the way of the Lord.

The Lord doesn't look at us all together, en masse. He looks each one of us in the face, in the eyes. His is not an abstract love, it is concrete. The Lord looks at me in a personal way. Letting ourselves be encountered by God means just this: letting ourselves be loved by God!

There is no occupation or social condition, no sin or crime of any kind, that could erase from the memory and the heart of God even one of His children.

How good it is for us when the Lord unsettles our lukewarm and superficial lives.

Whenever we encounter another person in love, we learn something new about God.

God manifests himself in historical revelation, in history. Time initiates processes, and space crystallizes them. God is in history, in the processes.

God created us so that we might live in a profound relationship of friendship with Him, and even when sin broke off this relationship with Him, with others, and with creation, God did not abandon us. The entire history of salvation is the story of God, who seeks out human beings, offers them His love, and welcomes them.

The love of God is not generic. God looks with love upon every man and woman, calling them by name.

Time is the messenger of God: God saves us in time, not in a moment. At times, He works miracles, but in everyday life He saves us through time. Sometimes we think that if the Lord comes into our life, He will change us. Yes, we do change: it is called conversion. But He does not act 'like a fairy with a magic wand.' No. He gives you the grace and He says, as He said to everyone He healed: 'Go, walk.'

The Lord loves us tenderly. The Lord knows the beautiful science of caresses—God's tendernesses. He does not love us with words. He approaches us, and in being close to us gives us His love with the deepest possible tenderness. More difficult than loving God is letting ourselves be loved by God.

I believe in God—not in a Catholic God; there is no Catholic God. There is God, and I believe in Jesus Christ, his incarnation. Jesus is my teacher and my pastor, but God, the Father, Abba, is the light and the Creator. This is my Being.

The Lord is knocking at the door of our hearts. Have we put a sign on the door saying: 'Do not disturb?'

The conscience is the interior place for listening to the truth, to goodness, for listening to God; it is the inner place of my relationship with Him, the One who speaks to my heart and helps me to discern, to help me understand the way I must take and, once the decision is made, to go forward, to stay faithful.

Have you thought about the talents God has given you? Have you thought how you can put them at the service of others? Do not bury your talents! Set your stakes on great ideals, the ideals that enlarge the heart, the ideals of service that make your talents fruitful. Life is not given to us to be jealously guarded for ourselves, but it is given to us so that we may give it in turn. Dear young people, have a deep spirit! Do not be afraid to dream of great things!

With God, nothing is lost; but without Him, everything is lost.

I would also like to say to anyone who feels far away from God and the Church, to anyone who is timid or indifferent, to those who think they can no longer change: the Lord calls you, too, to become part of His people, and He does this with great respect and love! He invites us to be part of this people, the people of God!

For this reason, to those who, today too, 'wish to see Jesus,' to those who are searching for the face of God; to those who received catechesis when they were little and then developed it no further and perhaps have lost their faith; to so many who have not yet encountered Jesus personally ... to all these people we can offer three things: *the Gospel, the Crucifix and the witness of our faith*, poor but

sincere. The Gospel: there we can encounter
Jesus, listen to Him, know Him. The Crucifix:
the sign of the love of Jesus who gave Himself
for us. And then a faith that is expressed in
simple gestures of fraternal charity. But mainly
in the coherence of life, between what we
say and what we do. Coherence between our
faith and our life, between our words and our
actions: Gospel, Crucifix, Witness.

The return to the sacred and the quest for spirituality which mark our own time are ambiguous phenomena. Today, our challenge is not so much atheism as the need to respond adequately to many people's thirst for God, lest they try to satisfy it with alienating solutions or with a disembodied Jesus who demands nothing of us with regard to others. Unless these people find in the Church a spirituality which can offer healing and liberation, and fill them with life and peace, while at the same time summoning them to fraternal communion and missionary fruitfulness, they will end up by being taken in by solutions which neither make life truly human nor give glory to God.

Allow yourselves to be surprised by God. Don't be frightened of surprises. They shake the ground from under your feet, and they make us unsure. But they move us forward in the right direction.

Ask yourselves this question: How often is Jesus inside and knocking at the door to be let out, to come out? And we do not let Him out because of our own need for security, because so often we are locked into ephemeral structures that serve solely to make us slaves and not free children of God.

Let the risen Jesus enter your life—welcome Him as a friend, with trust: He is life! If up till now you have kept Him at a distance, step forward. He will receive you with open arms. If you have been indifferent, take a risk; you won't be disappointed. If following Him seems difficult, don't be afraid. Trust Him, be confident that He is close to you, He is with you, and He will give you the peace you are looking for and the strength to live as He would have you do.

Do you allow yourselves to be gazed upon by the Lord? But how do you do this? You look at the tabernacle and you let yourselves be looked at … it is simple! 'It is a bit boring; I fall asleep.' Fall asleep then, sleep! He is still looking at you. But know for sure that He is looking at you!

And for this reason He (the Father) needs His child, He is waiting for Him, He loves Him, He looks for Him, He forgives Him, He wants Him close to Him, just as close as the hen who wants her chicks.

Our life is not given to us like an opera libretto, in which all is written down; but it means going, walking, doing, searching, seeing …We must enter into the adventure of the quest for meeting God; we must let God search and encounter us.

Christ's love and His friendship are not an illusion—Jesus on the cross shows how real they are—nor are they the privilege of the few. You will discover this friendship and feel its full fruitfulness and beauty if you seek it with sincerity, open yourselves to Him with trust, cultivate your spiritual life with perseverance, receiving the sacraments, meditating on Sacred Scripture, praying assiduously, and living with deep involvement in the Christian community.

Newness always makes us a bit fearful, because we feel more secure if we have everything under control, if we are the ones who build, program, and plan our lives in accordance with our own ideas, our own comfort, our own preferences ... The newness which God brings into our life is something that actually brings fulfillment, that gives true joy, true serenity, because God loves us and desires only our good.

What does obeying God mean? Does it mean that we must behave like slaves? No, whoever obeys God is free; he is not a slave! And how can this be? It seems like a contradiction ... The word 'obey' comes from Latin, and means to listen, to hear others. Obeying God is listening to God, having an open heart to follow the path that God points out to us. Obedience to God is listening to God, and it sets us free.

God is the light that illuminates the darkness, even if it does not dissolve it, and a spark of divine light is within each of us. In the letter I wrote to you, you will remember I said that our species will end but the light of God will not end and at that point it will invade all souls and it will all be in everyone.

PART NINE

Humility & Idolatry

Humility saves man: pride makes him lose his way.

If we are too attached to riches, we are not free. We are slaves.

No one can grow if he does not accept
his smallness.

Salvation cannot be bought or sold: it's a gift. It's given to us, it's free. We can't be saved through ourselves ... But in order to receive this salvation, we need a humble heart, a meek heart, an obedient heart. Like that of Mary. And the model for this road towards salvation is the same God, his Son, who didn't consider being equal to God an advantage which cannot be abandoned.

The humility of Christ was real, the decision to be small, to stay with other small people, with the excluded, to stay among us, all of us sinners. But be careful: this is not an ideology! It is a way of being and living that begins with love that starts from the heart of God.

Peace requires the force of meekness, the force of nonviolence, of truth and of love.

If one has the answers to all the questions—
that is the proof that God is not with him. It
means that he is a false prophet using religion
for himself. The great leaders of the people
of God, like Moses, have always left room for
doubt. You must leave room for the Lord, not
for our certainties; we must be humble.

May we learn to say 'thank you' to God and to one another. We teach children to do it, and then we forget to do it ourselves!

You can't govern without loving the people and without humility! And every man, every woman, who has to take up the service of government, must ask themselves two questions: 'Do I love my people in order to serve them better? Am I humble and do I listen to everybody, to diverse opinions, in order to choose the best path?' If you don't ask those questions, your governance will not be good. The man or woman who governs—who loves his people—is a humble man or woman.

A small step, in the midst of great human limitations, can be more pleasing to God than a life which appears outwardly in order but moves through the day without confronting great difficulties.

Humility, meekness, magnanimity, and love to preserve unity! These, these are the roads, the true roads of the Church. Let us listen to this again. Humility against vanity, against arrogance—humility, meekness, magnanimity, and love preserve unity.

God acts in humility, in silence, in the little things. This begins with Creation, where the Lord does not use 'a magic wand,' but creates man 'with mud.' It is a style that runs through the whole of salvation history.

The only way to escape corruption, the only way to overcome temptation to the sin of corruption, is service. Because corruption is pride, arrogance—and service humiliates you. It is 'humble charity to help others.'

We need to safeguard our smallness in order to have a personal dialogue with God. God always speaks to us on a personal level, using our names. It's never a dialogue between the powerful and the masses.

Idolatry, then, is always polytheism, an aimless passing from one lord to another. Idolatry does not offer a journey but rather a plethora of paths leading nowhere and forming a vast labyrinth.

It is so very sad to find a worldly Christian who is sure—according to him or her—of that security that the faith gives and of the security that the world provides. You cannot be on both sides. The Church—all of us—must strip herself of the worldliness that leads to vanity, to pride; that is idolatry.

Even today, there are so many idols, and even today there are so many idolaters, so many who think they are wise. But even among us, among Christians … they think they're wise, they know everything … They've become foolish and exchange the glory of the incorruptible God with an image: myself, my ideas, my comforts.

But since we all have need to worship—because we have the imprint of God within us—when we do not worship God, we worship creatures. And this is the passage from faith to idolatry.

God did not want there to be an idol at the center of the world, but rather that men and women bring the world ahead through their work.

But before all else we need to keep alive in our world the thirst for the absolute, and to counter the dominance of a one-dimensional vision of the human person, a vision which reduces human beings to what they produce and to what they consume: this is one of the most insidious temptations of our time.

When a society lacks God, even prosperity is joined by a terrible spiritual poverty.

Men and women are sacrificed to the idols of profit and consumption: it is the 'culture of waste.' If a computer breaks, it is a tragedy, but poverty, the needs and dramas of so many people, end up being considered normal. (...) When the stock market drops 10 points in some cities, it constitutes a tragedy. Someone who dies is not news, but lowering income by 10 points is a tragedy! In this way people are thrown aside as if they were trash.

If you hoard material possessions, they will rob you of your soul.

We are living in an information-driven society which bombards us indiscriminately with data—all treated as being of equal importance—and which leads to remarkable superficiality in the area of moral discernment. In response, we need to provide an education which teaches critical thinking and encourages the development of mature moral values.

There is the tendency to place ourselves and our ambitions at the center of our lives. This is very human, but it is not Christian.

In other parts of our society, we see the growing attraction to various forms of a 'spirituality of well-being' divorced from any community life, or to a 'theology of prosperity' detached from responsibility for our brothers and sisters, or to depersonalized experiences which are nothing more than a form of self-centeredness.

Once man has lost the fundamental orientation which unifies his existence, he breaks down into the multiplicity of his desires; in refusing to await the time of promise, his life-story disintegrates into a myriad of unconnected instants.

We should recognize how in a culture where each person wants to be bearer of his or her own subjective truth, it becomes difficult for citizens to devise a common plan which transcends individual gain and personal ambitions.

There exists, indeed, a sort of spiritual worldliness, which hides behind the appearance of piety and even love for the Church, and which leads to the pursuit, not of the glory of God, but rather of personal well-being.

When we do not adore God, we adore something else. Money and power are false idols which often take the place of God.

PART TEN

Forgiveness & Grace

A little bit of mercy makes the world less cold and more just.

The Lord never tires of forgiving. It is we who tire of asking for forgiveness.

'Well! Father, I am a sinner; I have tremendous sins. How can I possibly feel part of the Church?' Dear brother, dear sister, this is exactly what the Lord wants, that you say to him, 'Lord, here I am, with my sins.' Is one of you here without sin? Anyone? No one, not one of us. We all carry our sins with us. But the Lord wants to hear us say to him, 'Forgive me, help me to walk, change my heart!' And the Lord can change your heart. In the Church, the God we encounter is not a merciless judge but is like the Father in the Gospel parable. You may be like the son who left home, who sank to the depths, farthest from the Gospel. When you have the strength to say, 'I want to come home,' you will find the door open. God will come to meet you because he is always waiting for you—God is always waiting for you. God embraces you, kisses you and celebrates.

Mercy is the true power that can save humanity and the world from sin and evil.

The Lord always forgives everything! Everything! But if you want to be forgiven, you must set out on the path of doing good. This is the gift!

Confessing our sins may be difficult for us, but it brings us peace. We are sinners, and we need God's forgiveness.

In life we all make many mistakes. Let us learn to recognize our errors and ask forgiveness.

In those who make up the Church, pastors and faithful, there are shortcomings, imperfections, and sins. The Pope has these, too—and many of them; but what is beautiful is that when we realize we are sinners we encounter the mercy of God, who always forgives. Never forget it: God always forgives and receives us into his love of forgiveness and mercy.

Whenever anyone finds the courage to ask for forgiveness, the Lord does not let such a petition go unheard.

Jesus understands our weaknesses and sins; and he forgives us if we allow ourselves to be forgiven.

Dear brothers and sisters, let us not be closed to the newness that God wants to bring into our lives. Are we often weary, disheartened, and sad? Do we feel weighed down by our sins? Do we think that we won't be able to cope? Let us not close our hearts, let us not lose confidence, let us never give up: there are no situations which God cannot change, there is no sin which he cannot forgive if only we open ourselves to him.

If you have a weight on your conscience, if you are ashamed of so many things that you've done, stop for a moment, do not panic. Think about the fact that that Someone is waiting for you because He has never stopped remembering you—and this Someone is your Father, it is God Who waits for you!

Conversion is a grace; it is 'a visit from God.'

If we—all of us—accept the grace of Jesus Christ, He changes our heart and from sinners makes us saints. To become holy we do not need to turn our eyes away and look somewhere else, or have as it were the face on a holy card! No, no, that is not necessary. To become saints only one thing is necessary: to accept the grace that the Father gives us in Jesus Christ. There, this grace changes our heart. We continue to be sinners for we are weak, but with this grace which makes us feel that the Lord is good, that the Lord is merciful, that the Lord waits for us, that the Lord pardons us—this immense grace that changes our heart.

God's grace is always greater than the prayer which sought it. The Lord always grants more than what He has been asked: you ask Him to remember you, and He brings you into His Kingdom!

Grace is not part of consciousness; it is the amount of light in our souls, not knowledge nor reason.

Let us ask for the grace to live in the truth without hiding anything from the Lord and without hiding anything from ourselves.

Grace is not given to decorate life but rather to make us strong in life, giving us courage to go forward!

When the kingdom of God diminishes, one of the signs is that you lose the sense of sin. [But] salvation will not come from our cleverness, from our astuteness, from our intelligence in taking care of our affairs. Salvation will come through the grace of God and from the daily training we receive through cooperating with this grace.

Let us ask the Holy Spirit for the grace to admit that we are sinners. Sinners, yes, but not corrupt.

When we pray courageously, the God gives us the grace, but He also gives us Himself in the grace: the Holy Spirit, that is, Himself!

This is the way of the Lord: it is to worship God, to love God above all things and to love your neighbor. It's so simple, but so difficult! This can only be done with grace.

PART ELEVEN

*Human Dignity,
Suffering & Solidarity*

To live as true children of God means to love our neighbor and to be close to those who are lonely and in difficulty.

There is so much indifference in the face of suffering. May we overcome indifference with concrete acts of charity.

The *com-passion* of God, his suffering-with-us, gives meaning and worth to our struggles and our suffering.
(Explaining the Latin roots of the word.)

In many places, generally speaking, due to the economic humanism that has been imposed in the world, the culture of exclusion, of rejection, is spreading. There is no place for the elderly or the unwanted child; there is no time for that unwanted person in the street. At times, it seems that for some people, human relations are regulated by two modern 'dogmas': efficiency and pragmatism ... [Have] the courage to go against the tide of this culture. Be courageous!

It is not 'progressive' to try to resolve problems by eliminating a human life.

This is the struggle of every person: be free or be a slave.

Even if the life of a person has been a disaster, even if it is destroyed by vices, drugs, or anything else—God is in this person's life. You can, you must try to seek God in every human life. Although the life of a person is a land full of thorns and weeds, there is always a space in which the good seed can grow. You have to trust God.

Situations can change; people can change. Be the first to seek to bring good. Do not grow accustomed to evil, but defeat it with good.

Our faith in Christ, who became poor, and was always close to the poor and the outcast, is the basis of our concern for the integral development of society's most neglected members.

No one must say that they cannot be close to the poor because their own lifestyle demands more attention to other areas. This is an excuse commonly heard in academic, business, or professional, and even ecclesial, circles. While it is quite true that the essential vocation and mission of the lay faithful is to strive that earthly realities and all human activity may be transformed by the Gospel, none of us can think we are exempt from concern for the poor and for social justice.

The current crisis is not only economic and financial but is rooted in an ethical and anthropological crisis. Concern with the idols of power, profit, and money, rather than with the value of the human person, has become a basic norm for functioning and a crucial criterion for organization. We have forgotten and are still forgetting that over and above business, logic, and the parameters of the market is the human being; and that something is men and women in as much as they are human beings by virtue of their profound dignity: to offer them the possibility of living a dignified life and of actively participating in the common good. Benedict XVI reminded us that precisely because it is human, all human activity, including economic activity, must be ethically structured and governed (Encyclical Letter *Caritas in Veritate*, n. 36). We must return to the centrality of the human being, to a more ethical vision of activities and of human relationships, without the fear of losing something.

How I wish everyone had decent work! It is essential for human dignity.

Suffering is a call to conversion: it reminds us of our frailty and vulnerability.

We know how, in recent times, violence has produced an attempt to eliminate God and the divine from the horizon of humanity, and we feel the value of witnessing in our societies to the original openness to the transcendent that is inscribed in the human heart. In this, we also feel close to all men and women who, although

not claiming to belong to any religious tradition,
still feel themselves to be in search of truth,
goodness, and beauty—God's Truth, Goodness,
and Beauty—and who are our precious allies in
the effort to defend human dignity, in building
a peaceful coexistence between peoples, and in
carefully protecting creation.

Among the vulnerable for whom the Church wishes to care with particular love and concern are unborn children, the most defenceless and innocent among us. Nowadays efforts are made to deny them their human dignity and to do with them whatever one pleases, taking their lives and passing laws preventing anyone from standing in the way of this. Frequently, as a way of ridiculing the Church's effort to defend their lives, attempts are made to present her position as ideological, obscurantist, and conservative. Yet this defence of unborn life is closely linked to the defence of each and every other human right. It involves the conviction that a human being is always sacred and inviolable, in any situation and at every stage of development. Human beings are ends in themselves and never a means of resolving other problems.

The dignity of the human person and the common good rank higher than the comfort of those who refuse to renounce their privileges. When these values are threatened, a prophetic voice must be raised. Nor is peace 'simply the absence of warfare, based on a precarious balance of power; it is fashioned by efforts directed day after day towards the establishment of the ordered universe willed by God, with a more perfect justice among men.' In the end, a peace which is not the result of integral development will be doomed; it will always spawn new conflicts and various forms of violence.

[I]n our throwaway culture, in which what we do not need, we cast aside, leaving only those who consider themselves righteous, who feel pure, who feel clean—poor things!— this word, solidarity, risks being cancelled from the dictionary, because it is an inconvenient word, because it obliges us to look to others, and to give ourselves to others with love.

[C]harity is not a simple question of providing assistance, and far less a form of assistance for quieting consciences. No, that is not love, that is sales, that is business. Love is free. Charity and love are a life choice, a way of being, of living, it is the way of humility and solidarity.

We must walk united with our differences: there is no other way to become one. This is the way of Jesus.

[I]t is necessary, today more than ever, for us to educate ourselves in solidarity, rediscovering the value and meaning of this uncomfortable word which is so often set aside, and to turn it into the attitude that forms the basis of decisions made at a political, economic, and financial level, and of relations between people, populations, and nations.

Let us remember well, however, that whenever food is thrown out it is as if food were stolen from the table of the poor, from the hungry! I ask everyone to reflect on the loss and waste of food, to identify ways and approaches which, by seriously dealing with this problem, convey solidarity and sharing with the underprivileged.

We have to state, without mincing words, that there is an inseparable bond between our faith and the poor. May we never abandon them.

Paradoxically, in a moment in which globalization allows us to be informed of situations of need throughout the world, and to multiply exchanges and human relations, there appears to be a growing tendency towards individualism and inwardness, which leads to a certain attitude of indifference— at a personal, institutional, and State level— towards those who die of hunger and suffer as a result of malnutrition, as if it were an inescapable fact.

Those who live judging their neighbor, speaking ill of their neighbor, are hypocrites, because they lack the strength and the courage to look to their own shortcomings. The Lord does not waste many words on this concept.

Some members of the Christian community are called to engage in the political sphere, which is a high form of charity, as Paul VI said. But as a Church we all have a strong responsibility, and that is to sow hope through works of solidarity, always seeking to collaborate in the best way with the public institutions.

Like the Good Samaritan, may we not be ashamed of touching the wounds of those who suffer, but try to heal them with concrete acts of love.

It is not just petty love that we can offer one another, but something much more profound: it is a communion that renders us able to enter into the joy and sorrow of others and make them sincerely our own.

Jesus teaches us to not be ashamed of touching human misery, of touching his flesh in our brothers and sisters who suffer.

[T]he way to relate to others which truly heals instead of debilitating us, is a mystical fraternity, a contemplative fraternity. It is a fraternal love capable of seeing the sacred grandeur of our neighbor, of finding God in every human being, of tolerating the nuisances of life in common by clinging to the love of God, of opening the heart to divine love and seeking the happiness of others just as their heavenly Father does.

The Lord loves a cheerful giver. May we learn to be generous in giving, free from the love of material possessions.

To go out of ourselves and to join others is healthy for us. To be self-enclosed is to taste the bitter poison of immanence, and humanity will be worse for every selfish choice we make.

Today, when the networks and means of human communication have made unprecedented advances, we sense the challenge of finding and sharing a 'mystique' of living together, of mingling and encounter, of embracing and supporting one another, of stepping into this flood tide which, while chaotic,

can become a genuine experience of fraternity,
a caravan of solidarity, a sacred pilgrimage.
Greater possibilities for communication thus
turn into greater possibilities for encounter
and solidarity for everyone. If we were able
to take this route, it would be so good, so
soothing, so liberating and hope-filled!

[T]he Gospel tells us constantly to run the risk of a face-to-face encounter with others, with their physical presence which challenges us, with their pain and their pleas, with their joy which infects us in our close and continuous interaction.

Be active members! Go on the offensive! Play down the field, build a better world, a world of brothers and sisters, a world of justice, of peace, of fraternity, of solidarity. Play always on the offensive!

We need to help others to realize that the only way is to learn how to encounter others with the right attitude, which is to accept and esteem them as companions along the way, without interior resistance. Better yet, it means learning to find Jesus in the faces of others, in their voices, in their pleas. And learning to suffer in the embrace of the crucified Jesus whenever we are unjustly attacked or meet with ingratitude, never tiring of our decision to live in fraternity.

Many try to escape from others and take refuge in the comfort of their privacy or in a small circle of close friends, renouncing the realism of the social aspect of the Gospel. For just as some people want a purely spiritual Christ, without flesh and without the cross, they also want their interpersonal relationships provided by sophisticated equipment, by screens and systems which can be turned on and off on command.

We must recover the whole sense of gift, of gratuitousness, of solidarity. Rampant capitalism has taught the logic of profit at all costs, of giving to get, of exploitation without looking at the person … and we see the results in the crisis we are experiencing! This Home is a place that teaches charity, a 'school' of charity, which instructs me to go encounter every person, not for profit, but for love.

Beware of the temptation of jealousy! We are all in the same boat and headed to the same port! Let us ask for the grace to rejoice in the gifts of each, which belong to all.

I especially ask Christians in communities throughout the world to offer a radiant and attractive witness of fraternal communion. Let everyone admire how you care for one another, and how you encourage and accompany one another: 'By this everyone will know that you are my disciples, if you have love for one another' (Jn 13:35).

Human dignity is the same for all human beings: when I trample on the dignity of another, I am trampling on my own.

PART TWELVE

The Lessons of the Cross

From the cross, Christ teaches us to love even those who do not love us.

How beautiful it is to stand before the Crucifix, simply to be under the Lord's gaze, so full of love.

The Cross is the price of true love. Lord, give us the strength to accept and carry our crosses!

The Cross is the word through which God has responded to evil in the world. Sometimes it may seem that God does not react to evil, as if He is silent. And yet, God has spoken, He has replied, and His answer is the Cross of Christ: a word which is love, mercy, and forgiveness.

Jesus on the cross feels the whole weight of the evil, and with the force of God's love He conquers it; He defeats it with His resurrection. This is the good that Jesus does for us on the throne of the Cross. Christ's cross, embraced with love, never leads to sadness, but to joy, to the joy of having been saved and of doing a little of what He did on the day of His death.

What has the Cross given to those who have gazed upon it and to who have touched it? What has the Cross left in each one of us? You see, it gives us a treasure that no one else can give: the certainty of the faithful love which God has for us. A love so great that it enters into our sin and forgives it, enters into our suffering and gives us the strength to bear it. It is a love which enters into death to conquer it and to save us.

God placed on Jesus' cross all the weight of our sins, all the injustices perpetrated by every Cain against his brother, all the bitterness of the betrayal by Judas and by Peter, all the vanity of tyrants, all the arrogance of false friends. It was a heavy cross, like night experienced by abandoned people, heavy like the death of loved ones, heavy because it carries all the ugliness of evil. However, the Cross is also glorious like the dawn after a long night, for it represents all the love of God, which is greater than our iniquities and our betrayals. In the Cross we see the monstrosity of man, when he allows evil to guide him; but we also see the immensity of the mercy of God, who does not treat us according to our sins but according to his mercy.

J esus, with His cross, walks with us and takes upon Himself our fears, our problems, and our sufferings, even those which are deepest and most painful. With the Cross, Jesus unites Himself to the silence of the victims of violence, those who can no longer cry out, especially the innocent and the defenseless. The Cross of Christ bears the suffering and the sin of mankind, including our own. Jesus accepts all this with open arms, bearing on His shoulders our crosses and saying to us: 'Have courage! You do not carry your cross alone! I carry it with you. I have overcome death and I have come to give you hope, to give you life' (Jn 3:16).

About the Editor

Andrea Kirk Assaf has had the rare privilege of covering three pontificates in the span of a decade: the pontificates of John Paul II, Benedict XVI, and Francis. In 2002 she moved to Rome to write for *Inside the Vatican* magazine and several other Catholic and secular news outlets, covering World Youth Day in Toronto, the funeral of John Paul II, the election of Pope Benedict XVI, and now the popularity of the first successor of St. Peter from the New World, Pope Francis. Along with her editor-journalist-translator husband, Tony Assaf, and their three children, Andrea divides her days between the Eternal City of Rome, Italy, and a rural homestead in Remus, Michigan, U.S.A.